About the Author

Israel L. Monzon Gonzalez is the author of the *A Voice Cried Out In The Concrete Wilderness*, a collection of poetry which depicted the creative assertion of an artist finding his voice. He is an avid sports fan who runs the baseball blog, Izzy's Baseball Diamond and a non-sports blog called Lost In Thought. He lives in Toronto where he uses the backdrop of a large, cosmopolitan city to absorb sources of inspiration for his poetry, and other literary endeavours.

Returning From Exile

Israel L. Monzon Gonzalez

Returning From Exile

Olympia Publishers
London

www.olympiapublishers.com
OLYMPIA PAPERBACK EDITION

Copyright © Israel L. Monzon Gonzalez 2024

The right of Israel L. Monzon Gonzalez to be identified as author of this work has been asserted in accordance with sections 77 and 78 of the Copyright, Designs and Patents Act 1988.

All Rights Reserved

No reproduction, copy or transmission of this publication
may be made without written permission.
No paragraph of this publication may be reproduced,
copied or transmitted save with the written permission of the publisher,
or in accordance with the provisions
of the Copyright Act 1956 (as amended).

Any person who commits any unauthorized act in relation to
this publication may be liable to criminal
prosecution and civil claims for damage.

A CIP catalogue record for this title is
available from the British Library.

ISBN: 978-1-80439-709-1

This is a work of fiction.
Names, characters, places and incidents originate from the writer's imagination. Any resemblance to actual persons, living or dead, is purely coincidental.

First Published in 2024

Olympia Publishers
Tallis House
2 Tallis Street
London
EC4Y 0AB

Printed in Great Britain

Dedication

To those returning from exile.

Foreword

The last three years and change have seemed to many like a strange form of exile. It is not quite forty years milling about in the desert nor seventy in some strange land, dragged along against your will; and yet, it cuts deeply. You feel robbed of something that one could never replace or rebuild. Time is unique like that. Money, love, knowledge and things can be rebuilt or replaced but time cannot. Once time is lost it is lost, permanently. It has this unforgiving finality to it. A Mexican song describes time as a cruel friend. As we emerge from the lockdowns, the hospital wards, the solitary confinement that we once called home, this description seems ever more apt.

For those of my generation, the sense of loss is particularly acute. The older generations had their youth in full. The children will hopefully still have theirs. But we, the lucky ones, the privileged, we will have this hole, this sense that our youth was stunted, short-circuited. Us twenty-somethings, we who must mould the post-pandemic world, must live with the loss of the illusions of our twenties as an old Swiss song calls them. Those of us in our late twenties in particular must now confront the imminent loss of a youth that was never fully ours. When you read this, my twenties will be sand sifting through my hands. Perhaps there will no longer be sand to gently grate my palms. My youth will be gone. I will have climbed down from Sugar Mountain with its coloured balloons into the portal of maturity. I will not be young anymore but I will not yet be old. My time will be short but perhaps not as short as it seems. Or perhaps it indeed is and I must hurry. Time, with its uniquely harsh sense of legalism will pass its verdict.

And yet, not all is gloom. Other generations have lost more and still achieved great things. The generation that defeated Hitler, Mussolini and Tojo lost five years and yet became the greatest of all. Their parents, who lived through the first great war and the previous pandemic nurtured this heroic generation. Perhaps, we too are being moulded for our own heroic struggle. Perhaps, we are the generation tasked with navigating the world order altering events that seem to occur once or twice a century.

As we emerge from exile in our rooms we emerge to a world that looks different from the one we left behind. Life costs more, Europe is in flames again, hunger menaces the developing world, basics like baby formula are luxuries in the world's richest nation. We emerge into a world on the brink; brink of war, brink of famine, brink of social breakdown. Initially, it seems foreign. We've become used to life on screens and the dangers seem distant. Yet, they circle us like Tamerlane's hordes of centuries past. Camus said of his generation that its task was to ensure that the world did not destroy itself. Perhaps ours is similarly tasked. Just maybe, it is our brush with destiny to crush the Hitler and Mussolini of our times and save for another generation at least, the democratic system in which we grew up. And perhaps it is our lot to improve it, rendering it fairer and more representative of all. Maybe this exile was meant to shape us for a greater mission than that which our parents were tasked with undertaking.

Circling back to poetry, this collection is not necessarily meant to predict the future or even profess any kind of socio-political doctrines. Instead, it is meant to give voice to the existential angst of my generation and the conflicting ideas about the way our once relatively cozy reality has changed. The goal is to speak for a generation. I am no longer content to merely win the creative victory of which I spoke in my previous collection *A Voice Cried Out In The Concrete Wilderness*. This collection has a higher purpose. It must reflect a greater sense of maturity, a more realistic view of the world and the struggles of the people within it.

I would submit that struggle is the overriding theme of this new collection. Much of human history can be summed up in this eight-letter word whose connotations are overwhelmingly negative. And yet, there is a life-affirming spin on it. As long as we struggle we are alive. As long as we struggle, we will need to engineer and invent. As long as we struggle, there will always be a need to creatively express feelings and ideas. And so here I am, standing at the ready to do just that.

There are many types of struggles and therefore many different types of pieces. There will no doubt be pieces about the geopolitical struggle between freedom and tyranny, between oppressed and oppressor. But there will also be pieces about other, more subtle forms of struggle.

For example, there will necessarily be examinations on struggles of love. Gentlemen, you know all about the girl or girls that got away because we were overcome in our silent struggle with our self-esteem or with the more embarrassing struggle in getting our tongues, windpipes and brains to function around her. You probably remember all too well the romantic walks on the beach that happened in some far-flung corner of your mind. And what to say of that pillow you clung fast to in the dead of night that in some alternate reality was her. Oh, and those melancholy games of Solitaire on Saturday night as you composed the most beautiful song that she would never hear. And yes, the torturous love songs that constantly remind you of your loss of something that was never yours to begin with.

And what of those who did chance upon a lover only to wind up more alone than if they had been left alone? Do they not struggle? Do they not mourn the freedom of yesteryear? Do they not feel trapped in a toxic cycle of fights, sarcasm and obscenities? I wonder if they envy those of us who are single.

There are other personal struggles to be examined as well. Many have lost loved ones without so much as being able to properly say goodbye. They are left with a memory of their loved one desperate for something as abundant as air. This is the final image. This is the mental scar with which they struggle. The survivors must go on, but for many the burden of guilt is great, and not all can suffer the struggle. They are left to wrestle with a cosmic sense of injustice, of confusion, of failure. They committed no crime but yet they feel they must do the time.

Others still have lost their livelihoods. They watch helplessly as the cupboards grow steadily emptier, their children thinner and their prospects slimmer. Time and again they dress up and rehearse their lines. Time and again the door gets slammed in their faces. "The job market's hot" they're told. But for them there is no smoke. And so, they live a life ever more dependent on the whims of politicians sequestered in their mansions, cabinets stocked generously with chardonnay. They lose the car, the house and even the spouse. And so, they join the under-bridge debate society, conducting their filibusters in graffiti format aimed at the government, society or some higher power. Every day is the same; passers-by, the cops, the rain, the cold, as each day they grow a touch more old and a touch more cold.

There are existential struggles too, those troublesome questions that lurk just under the surface of the mind. *"Is life really just school, graduate then subway, work, subway, home, rinse, repeat? What was the point of that expensive degree anyway? Do you chase your dreams or do you take society's advice to do something steady and stable? You come to question where the years went and what exactly you achieved. And now, as we emerge from the plague, there is the process of becoming human again. Cue relearning the familiar behaviours of handshakes, smiles, small-talk and happy hour. Does it even matter? Do people even care about those things anymore? Regarding the state of the world, are we headed for nuclear war? What's the next virus that will grind the world to a halt? Is economic collapse imminent?"* These things bring us to question if there's even a point in chasing dreams, chasing love, chasing money etc. And so, we struggle with the latent sense of impending doom and what to do about it. We wrestle with cowardly optimism versus heroic pessimism. We drown in the ink of mutually contradictory self-help books in search of direction. We hide in feel-good pseudo-truisms to shelter ourselves from reality. We develop escape mechanisms from the dour reality in which we live but even so the struggle continues.

There are other struggles no doubt which I will not expound on. The subject is heavy and I hope you will be left with the energy to read the poems themselves. I am not a believer in long forewords that are almost the same length as the work itself. Suspense is good but not that good. I also do not want the foreword to be a struggle to get through. There is enough struggle ahead. I hope that there will also be a rewarding experience ahead that will provide interesting insights on life and on the challenges that our generation will be entrusted with as the 21st century comes of age and we begin giving shape to the world future generations will inherit.

Section One:
The Struggles of Love

The preeminent form of struggle in human existence is that which concerns a simple four-letter word called love. It is amazing to me that such a simple word can so completely dominate human thought across cultures, nationalities and art forms. It is a word that can encompass feelings towards anyone but much human angst, much human struggle, concerns itself with one specific form of love. It is this form of love which will inform the struggle-infested poetry which you will soon be subjected to.

Romantic love is that stupor-like, irrational state which the vast majority of humanity will experience at some point or another. Even the aromantics cannot count themselves as having fully escaped its grasp. After all, any trip to the store, the mall or the ballpark will confront them with a small cross-section of the love songs that make up the immense majority of modern pop music. Everywhere we go, we find ourselves swarmed in some form or another by that which begets the most beautiful form of struggle. The forms which romantic struggles will take in our individual lives can vary as wildly as one's moods whilst under the sway of a romantic episode. This implies that the romantic struggle is fertile ground for artists, musicians and of course, poets.

What are some of these struggles? Well, consider the

predicament of the terminally shy man who continually disqualifies himself from finding the love of his life. He is not morally squalid. He is not indolent. He is erudite. Perhaps, he is even good-looking, whatever that term means.

And yet, he is fatally insecure, self-conscious, inarticulate, boring even. Through no fault of his own, his existence is scarcely acknowledged by those whose affection he pines for the most. He devours self-help books and articles in search of answers. He picks himself apart looking for the reasons for which girls continually ignore him or relegate him where romantic dreams go to die. (the friend zone) As he does so, rather than alleviate his ailments, his heightened awareness of his many flaws only serves to throw him into deeper into the maelstrom of self-doubt and self-loathing that informs his shyness and his bumbling delivery wherever he does dare approach the latest love of his life. As the years pass, he becomes further frustrated and either gives up completely or turns himself into a counterfeit of some other man and in so doing condemns himself to a cacophony of dysfunctional, inauthentic and unfulfilling relationships.

The hopeless romantic also features another struggle and this concerns his relationship with reality. All who fall in love develop an absurdly idealized view of their prospective significant other but the hopeless romantic, I can assure you, is especially prone to this sort of romantic masochism. He paints in his mind a picture of someone devoid of flaws, however trivial. This person becomes the personification of every beautiful love song, the subject of his amateurish love poetry that expresses the absurd idealization of this particular person. (I am not much of a love poet myself so this would include me should I fall into such a situation) The hopeless romantic trades the possibilities of the real world for a parallel life in which he walks hand in hand with this impossibly perfect human and their cherubim-like offspring in some idyllic park with the most perfect cup of coffee in hand. Surely he works, does chores, maybe even works assiduously on his personal projects but his mind always drifts to her. He lives in a permanent state of low-level slumber, so intimately connected to and yet so irredeemably sequestered from the ravages of everyday life where this perfect lover of his is but another toxic human like himself with warts and flaws, probably worse than his own. If he ever snaps out of it, there he goes with his withdrawal symptoms like a junkie. If he does not, then I suppose he lives two lies, (or should I say lives) as opposed to one so perhaps not all is bad.

Successfully entering a relationship is also no refuge from the romantic struggles. Many relationships are sorry spectacles of toxicity. They are codependent, distant, hot-cold, abusive or simply unfulfilling for whatever assortment of reasons. I would even question if entering a relationship is any kind of success at all in spite of how society paints it. It seems to me that entering a relationship is merely consigning yourself to an endless winter of struggles encompassing the physical and the emotional. And yet, if managed correctly by two sane adults, the struggles can produce something beautiful and be something beautiful in their own right. I can attest to such a thing as the product of a stable, successful relationship between two sane people who did not turn their love into some kind of Panglossian delusion nor an absurd competition of egos nor an amateur debate club.

But the reality is that many relationships are not like this.

Otherwise, divorce lawyers would be polishing their resumes en masse. Houses are not homes, nor bedrooms, nor dream chambers. Lovers are tormented by doubts. "Is he seeing another woman?" "Does she still love me?" There are egos to be satisfied. There are insecurities to be soothed. There are relationships that are simply shallow, rooted in sex, checking an item off the bucket list or some other flimsy foundation. Romantic love in my generation resembles a game more than a commitment to another human being. Divorce rates are the highest they have ever been. The criteria many people have for picking a partner is steadily becoming more vacuous. Rather than pick a partner based on actually important qualities such as empathy, intelligence, ability to compromise and so forth, we pick exclusively based on money, looks, or worse still, the sense that there is nothing else available. Naturally, what we see around us is seemingly a hundred failed relationships for every successful one. Maybe this is only perception but this still counts for something. Even long-lasting relationships cannot necessarily be thought of as successful. Many choose to stay trapped out of a pathological fear of being alone because society wrongly teaches us that there is something wrong with being alone. Single and free always beats hitched and trapped. And yet, society seems to preach the opposite.

In the end, love is fertile ground for struggles whether you have had your flings or are still rummaging through articles explaining how you are supposed to find a partner. Whether you are a player, a coquette, a hopeless romantic or an aromantic, you will find yourself struggling with romantic love in some way or another. You see, love is the ultimate struggle! The poet relishes this fact as struggle is a perfect subject to examine poetically. This is what we will now do without further delay.

Angel

Angel
Burn me in the fire of your sun-kissed glow
Fly me through the clouds
Take me through the waters where the fair winds blow
Hear the words of the wind
When he tells you that we're meant to be

Angel
Kiss me till a love song comes to life for me
Let the sparkles fly
Colouring the dark grey hued reality
There's no point asking why
We gotta go all out 'cause this life's too short

Angel
Connect to the domain where the loving grows
Kiss a kiss goodnight
As we bid adieu on this starry night
Reap what the feeling sows
Let it bloom into a dream world for two

The Moonlit Room

You waltz into the master's chamber
With the magic that brings him to you
He enters a world he never knew
And never mind the danger
Not a care that love's a stranger

Love, you've wrapped him in the darkness of your soul
You tie him to his captain's chair
Free him from the bonds he wore
And you give him brand new clothes to wear
For you've shown him to be fully bare
You've eaten him whole from skin to core
You know him for the beggar that he is

There's danger in the moonlit room
You've caught a man within your truth
He's tried the apple of his eye
And he knows that he's condemned to die
But first he must infect you with his truth
Yes, first he must infect you with his truth

You're a prisoner of the moonlit room
Master and slave at once
Insane and sane
Aladdin Sane

Rubbing fast in hopes of smoke
You're wetter than the driving rain
And then it seems the genie finally rose

It's silent since the dream was dreamed
You crash into reality
You're back to vapid vanity
He puts you back into the world
In hopes that you'll recall who twirled
Your passions in the moonlit room

Forever Beautiful

You lie there still sleeping
Weaving worlds and dreaming
I can only wonder where you've gone
The moon pours its light on your illusions
I look at you dreaming
Forgive my intrusions

Forever beautiful
Forever beautiful
Where you go I go
And I won't be long

Forever beautiful
Forever beautiful
Where you go I go
And I won't be long
Yes I won't be long

A life lived in silence upon your pillow
Where you flew like a willow
With a lover in hand
To some distant new land
That I never knew of
In search of a new love
That I wish I knew of

Forever beautiful
Forever beautiful
Where you go I go
And I won't be long

Forever beautiful
Forever beautiful
Where you go I go
And I won't be long
Yes I won't be long

There's rarified air in every mountain
There's crystal clear water in every fountain
And so, there's tenderness still waiting for me
And so, there's a new world still waiting for me

Forever beautiful
Forever beautiful
Where you go I go
And I won't be long

Forever beautiful
Forever beautiful
Where you go I go
And I won't be long
Yes I won't be long

Sappho and the Poet

The poet gets into his verse
In a meter that is only hers
He writes sonnets that she never reads
Of a love that to forever leads
She's a passer-by without goodbye
Her view cast to the big, blue sky
No time for poor, poem pushers in love

She subtly plays a leading role
In a Broadway play she doesn't know
She's burnt a gaping hole
In a man she doesn't know
She is shadow to his human
Always there and yet elusive
His words ever more effusive
For his goddess dressed in human

He cries tears of ink on crumpled sheets
Reddened by the blood he bleeds
As the papers cut still deeper
Towards the heart that hardly beats

From all the warnings that he never heeds
Of giving hearts to passers-by without goodbye
His castles rest upon the sky
That slowly tumbles down

He blurs dream and reality
While she labours in insanity
He is swept in the delusion
His life naught but an illusion
She cares not for biting apples
There is poison all around her
There are judges with their gavels
Hammering her will to love her

She is Sappho with a pencil skirt
Lipstick, pumps and painted toes
Who she wants to know, she only knows
There are questions on the guys she knows
The sand pours in the hourglass
There are grated souls and grated wills
Beneath her iron will a heart of glass
A victim of the kind of love that kills

She's a lover of a Grecian kind
Goes from below up to the mind
Both sides want a white night bled with her
But to the left she softly turns As the moans and groans take over her
They grate her with the love that burns
While the poet's left to sweep the ashes far
And to melt away in embers not his own

The poet gets into his verse
In a meter that is only hers
A broken cry as the curtain falls
Upon the happy ending dreamed
In his stupors that he never streamed
He's just left with his four walls
To pen for a passer-by without goodbye
A helpless little poem asking why

Esther and Ashuerus

Esther play me like your fiddle
Make believe that you're in love with me
That it's meant to be
And hide the truth far, far away
Hidden from the sunlight of the day

Esther paint a web of lies
Lead me to your pirate paradise
Are you mine to hold
Or were those just pretty lies you told
To make me feel that love would come my way

Esther dance me to delusion
Reality be trumped by the illusion
That we're meant to be
And that all your future dances are for me
It's your strings that vibrate in my soul

Queen Janine

If you ever loved my love
You'd dream of her when the nights run cold
She can take you to heaven with a gentle touch
You never knew you could ask for so much
And if she should ever disappear
You'd keep on searching through to the end of the world
Hoping to find your Queen Janine

The forests sing songs of love that she taught them to sing
The streams and the winds sing in perfect harmony of the way things must be
Enchanted trails and the old travails that gave birth to love
And if it should ever die young
You'd keep on crying through to the end of the world
Until you die for Queen Janine

The winters are colder and you want her warmth more
Snowflakes are sculpted with the smile on her face
Her hair tickles your face as you sit by the fire
And if she should tell you a joke
You'd keep on laughing through to the end of the world
With love in your heart for Queen Janine

Gifts at Night

Gifts at night give such delight
A reassuring, slow hand
Poetry murmured in the dead of night
Into her tickled, anxious ear
As you hold her cool, frail hand
Lovingly clutching what you hold dear
Nobody watching
Just the two of you

Gently, softly you sing her a song
A new number in your canon
Inspired by a need to belong
Making magic as you love Rhiannon
Under the full moon's watch
Your bodies erupt in song

Neither dares to break the spell
Of a magic more black than white
More naughty than nice
But you to each other bring light

You are shameless dancers in the moonlight
Performing wizardry on your bodies
Hoping to paralyze time itself
Dreading the morning church bell
As you lose yourself in her
And her in you, oh so completely

She thanks you profusely, profoundly
For coming unashamed to her
Bearing gifts at night

Of Dreamers and Lovers

Of dreamers and lovers, it can safely be said
The night leaves them feeling dead in bed
Reeling and keeling over
From the rush in their heads
As the moon watches faithfully over
The lovers and dreamers fixed to their beds

Of dreamers and lovers it can safely be said
They went where the muse of their passions led
No fears and no regrets later
They tasted the heights of pleasure
Living life at their leisure
Knowing the world could wait for later

An Unrequited Love Letter

Light bursts through the darkness
Whenever you are near
You are seated here
Dressed in beauty and tenderness
Smelling of lilac and lavender
Oh, happy day in the calendar

Your voice, tender and melodious
Your hair, flowing like the falls
Falling for you, the sweetest of falls
Hard yet soft
Peaceful yet beautiful
Or perhaps I am merely delirious

Your walk, so elegant and graceful
A subtle dance only for me
Or so I wish
That would be wonderful
Oh, what wonderful life that would be

At night stars do shine
But not quite like your eyes
They have a special twinkle
Especially as the day slowly dies

You are the finest wine
My gentle fire on a winter's night
Playful warmth when the ground is white
The most majestic ferry on the Rhine
In the ocean blue of Bora Bora
The colourful chaos the Amazon
The ancient pride of the Parthenon
You are there
My beautiful, unwitting companion

If fate should deliver you into my arms
Let the robins sing songs
And the stars sparkle

And if fate should smile on another
Thank you all the same
For the kind reminder
That there is beauty in this world

Fly by Night

Jump on the jet plane with me
Feel the joy of being alive
Fly by night with me
High above the clouds we fly

We'll run away to anywhere
Our secret place nestled in infinity
Awash in our shared humanity
In a place where the winds blow fair

Let's sail away to eternity
Where water shimmers like sheets of gold
Adrift in beautiful insanity
Wishing to never grow old

Pilot and co-pilot
Hand in hand and heart in heart
Taking off
Ready to fly by night

Good Morning Beautiful

Good morning beautiful
The sun shines to flatter you
Birds sing you songs of love
While I simply go on mute
But the twinkle in eyes gives it away
I love you darling
Deeply, madly, passionately

If love were a melody
It would be your voice
If love were a river
It would be your flowing hair
And if love were a dream
It would be that first kiss
Played in my mind a million times

The joy of innocence is in your smile
The colours of the rainbow in your fingernails
Shimmering light on the lake mimics your eyes
And pardon my stargazing
But you just shine so bright
The spell is simply too strong
Gracefully wrapping me in your magic

How wonderful life would be

Tangled in each other's arms
Close the beating of each other's hearts
A perfect morning
Of hummingbirds and fresh made coffee
And three short words
Good morning beautiful

The Friend

Her eyes shine like the sun
Music is her voice
Could she be the one
Or is she another's to hold

If I write her a rhapsody
Will she ever hear
Why is she so far
Though I am so near

Is she mine to love
Or does another play her a melody
Where she is raptured in reverie
Does she know unrequited love

Am I where friends go to die
Does she even know my name
Will we swear love till we die
Take an oath before The Name

Death And The Mermaid

They say that you're the fall of man
Death to all that is strong and true
Many men have drowned for chasing you
So say the books of man

You've danced them to the depths below
Till their glory was fallen low
And as they breathed their last
It is to your body that they held fast

Underwater girl
In depths of love you bathe
Death must be for you so hard to give

Underwater girl
Forever in your depth
Men who lust for love

They say that you're Bathsheba's child
Temptress of sailors and kings
Who made killers of virtuous kings
That wished to leave you with child

You've bent their swords and smashed their thrones
Repossessed everything that they own

As they drowned in your charms
Cut down by your beautiful arms

Underwater girl
Enchanted men do swim
Death must be for you so hard to give

Underwater girl
Drenched with passions deep
Men who lust for love

They say you're the wicked queen
Killing softly with your kiss
When the coral snake does hiss
No choice but to drown in love

You've cleared them out and burnt them out
Left adrift to a watery death
And still with their last breath
They murmured out your name

Underwater girl
They fly and then they die
Death must be for you so hard to give

Underwater girl
Immortal you must stay
I just meant to say… I love you

Death Of A Summer Love

The weather turned colder
The night fell faster
And I felt a chill inside
Of one left to freeze outside
Eyes are not needed
When all can be seen by the heart
Eyes are not needed
When I can feel us drifting apart

Flowers once bloomed for you and me
The sun shined a path for you and me
But summer slowly turned to fall
Then snow answered Jack Frost's call
And I felt you slip-sliding away
No longer giving me your time of day
Gone was our star-gazing at night
Our once raging fire, a faintly flickering light

As the ball dropped to the ground
You were no longer around
No midnight kiss for you and me
There's you and me where there once was we

Our lives drifted apart
And the universe ordered itself again
All that's left is a broken heart
Of broken man left lonely once again

Eva And Her Garden

Eva tempts me into her garden
Lush as can be and full of grace
As only she can be
Absurd in her beauty
Disarming in her charm
Ready to spread her wings and fly

First she tempts my body
Then my heart and then my soul
And I have no recourse but to fall
Now I understand the fall of man
Into the deepest pit of love

I wish to slither into her garden
To eat of her fruit
To be the apple of her eye
Live a sliver of perfection
A slice of heaven
Locked in body and heart
Eternally and forevermore

Nabokov's Butterfly

A tear escaped from her eye
As Nabokov caught a butterfly
Lolita lollied about for her lover
Hungry for her Humbert Humbert
Bumper and bumper was his harvest
As he thrust himself deeper into her life
Hoping to make of her his wife
The answer to the puzzle loomed
As her rose slowly bloomed
Chess pieces were arranged perfectly
As his grazed her delicately
And slowly she learned to fly
Spreading her wings like a butterfly
Tip-toeing towards her lover
Toes en pointe like Nijinksy
Flying to the heavens
Like the Firebird of Igor Stravinsky

The Way We Were

Rock 'n' roll was in its infancy
Our brains were only in our heads
Sex wasn't synonymous with intimacy
No giant tower over our heads

Feelings were felt in jukeboxes
One dime at a time
Songs perfectly crafted in rhyme
For lovers and sly little foxes

No domes in the northern sky
No sharp spire to its side
Piercing into the heavens
Just a shoulder on which to cry

You were the most beautiful girl in school
And I, the starting quarterback
Both starry eyed, dream filled fools
Blessed were the fools

Remember the brown and red streetcars
The groovy people on Yonge and Bloor
There we were, the rich and poor
Lovers and vagabonds in the dive bars

Remember "It's Happening!"
All night dancing and prancing
And "Let's go, go, go" on our radio
Music and news on our radio

Life was slow and fast all at once
Fast times at Maple Leaf Gardens
Slow times at the prom dance
Lovers making their way into the magic gardens

That's the way we were
Jazzy, groovy and carefree
Musical, lyrical and comical
That's the way we were

Today we are old and broken
Creaky, croaky and cranky
But we can say we lived
Oh, what a life we lived

We loved and were loved
We became one with each other
Our love grew like the tower
And filled our hearts like a great lake

We can be proud
We can smile and sing out loud
For who we are and were
For the way we were

Section Two: Our Historic Struggles

In the over three thousand years of recorded history, we have been at peace for only a tiny sliver of that time, and even this is relative. Human history is one of war, starvation, terror and tragedy. From Megiddo and Qadesh to Ukraine and Syria in our time, we the masses have been pawns in a continual game of Risk-taking place between the powers of whatever era we have happened to live in. There are pestilences, economic collapses, dramatic geopolitical shifts and world order altering conflicts. This is our story. It is also our future. In other words, our story is one of struggle, both against each other and against tragic circumstances beyond our control.

From the first moment that a weapon was picked up in anger, man's interaction with man has largely followed a might makes right dynamic. As a result, history has largely been moulded by the powerful and unscrupulous. Alexander, Caesar and Napoleon were not moral giants. Their exploits were manifested in territorial gains on a map but also bodies left on the battlefield by their thousands. Their morality was that of the sword, their epistles, the battering ram, their credo, the cannon. They were products of a world in which the strong conquered and the weak perished. We remain subject to such a dynamic even with the comforting delusions provided by organizations such as the United Nations. Some like the Chinese regime conquer through debt and subversion. Others like the Russian regime conquer by the missile launcher with none able or willing to stop them save for those directly defending their homes. Might makes right continues to inform the struggle of nations today to stay alive. Today, Ukraine bears witness to this truth. Tomorrow it may be Taiwan.

Even the noble among us must be prepared to shed blood to stop the excesses of tyrants who were allowed to go too far. Hitler was stopped only through the total military defeat of the Germans. This cost the lives of millions. Similarly, Imperial Japan was stopped through the most terrible of all weapons known to man today. And yet, the alternative was perhaps more terrible, if only less dramatic. An invasion of the Japanese home islands would have perhaps cost as many or even more lives albeit over a larger period of time. Closer to our time, a second Shoah has only been prevented by a Jewish state prepared to use overwhelming military force to incapacitate those who would wish to follow Hitler's example. It has happened again and again. The genocide in the Balkans was stopped through NATO air power.

Another 9/11 has been prevented thus far by the neutralization of terrorist leaders. Conversely, an unwillingness to use military force allowed crises in Rwanda and Syria to degenerate into genocide. Today, our continued stated unwillingness to confront Putin's Russia has led to disaster in Eastern Europe and a world on the brink of total war which would be more brutal than any before it. Herein lies another struggle. Does the threat of a larger disaster a priori justify violence? Must we always stand ready to use violence to defend our homes and lives or is this morally abhorrent? What if the answer to both of those questions is yes? And if it is no must we then be prepared to accept subjugation at the hands of the cruellest of regimes where our brothers, sisters, spouses etc. will face torture and death? What if the basic tenet of world affairs, might makes right, forces us to choose between two morally squalid options? Can we even change that core tenet at all, or is it simply baked into the fabric of human consciousness?

Another point to make about our shared history and our shared future is that history has a certain predictive quality. Consider it a type of intellectual clairvoyance. What I mean to say is that looking at our past often winds up illuminating our future, especially given that we humans are so good at repeating the same mistakes again and again in new contexts. For example, we see the same pattern repeating from the last century of weak appeasers in the democratic west allowing dictators to push the envelope to the point that the world reaches a critical and deadly inflection point. We also see these same dictators becoming seduced by their own propaganda and venturing into conflicts that become the beginning of their end. Of course, before such a time comes, millions of lives and livelihoods have been destroyed. The years progress linearly but history has a cyclical quality to it with the same destructive errors and toxic character traits marking the leaders that lead at any given point in time. Sure, there is progress but technological advances and improved scientific know-how do not change basic human instincts. When in positions of power, we are no less arrogant, deceitful, abusive and outright cruel than our forefathers were. We just manifest it differently. We now know how to be more sophisticated about bamboozling the masses. The tools exist now also to exercise ever tighter control over citizens. Just look at China today.

Our future will be authoritarian regimes trying to destroy the liberal democratic order that exists today. It will also be unscrupulous men in the west seeking to capitalize on crises and a lagging confidence in our democratic institutions to cement their own power, as absolute as time and the popular will would allow them to. Again, weak and shortsighted leaders in the west will lead us to the brink of a world order altering conflict that will further hasten the breakdown of social order. Again, our failure to demand more of those we elect will be to blame. Again, we will respond to crises by electing demagogues and by further polarizing ourselves making it easier for Caesars in waiting to divide us Just like our ancestors before, we will find ourselves having to rebuild a broken and battered world.

And still, we will fight on, building and re-building property and lives. There is beauty in our collective struggle. In spite of it all, we continue to live and the verses of poets around the world bear witness to this triumph over adversity. For all the death, hatred and misery in the world, the poet always reminds us that beauty and insight always seep through the cracks.

Democracy Is Dead!

Democracy is dead and the democrats killed it
Republicanism is dead and the republicans killed it
Society falls to pieces
Shattered like the dreams of my broken heart

The sun is setting
Winter is coming
The summer is over
And we won't be saved

Freedom's on life support
Dictating a will to never be executed
The founding fathers wept
The liberty bell shattered

And so, my mood grew darker
I miss the world of my youth
When there were dreams to dream
And lovers to love

But now all is darkness
Red, black, grey
Devilishly forlorn
As if the sun went black

Aethelstan We Stan

Morning rose across the English sky
Above the thousands set to die
A confederation of three kings
Set to duel the great king
The Bretwalder!

A man called Aethelstan
Ruler of the English
Consecrated one of Wessex

Line by line
They formed for battle
Drums and bugles sounded
Steadily louder to the beat of the march
The hearts swordsmen pounded
As they approached the appointed place

Horses neighed as they prepared to gallop
Spears pointed to deadliest effect
Swords unsheathed in preparation to kill
And contact!
Hammers and axes giving a wallop
Bodies falling left and right at will
Green fields red with blood

Legs, arms, guts and brains litter the field

If they were earls or peasants I do not know
Princes and paupers fell
Left and right they fell
But it was the Bretwalder who gave chase
Thousands of the coalition lost their race
Behold!
A great slaughter!

As dusk announced itself Drums began to beat again
First quiet then steadily louder
Louder!
LOUDER!

And the surviving Saxons broke out in chorus
"Aethelstan we stan!"
"AETHELSTAN WE STAN!"
"AETHELSTAN WE STAN!"

The Battle Of Britain

You were shot out of the sky
One could say you were meant to die
Wrapped in flames the plane goes down
Covered in danger you pray your last

Stukas and Hurricanes dot the sky
Hundreds of birds will die
Shot down over Westminster
Crashing down over Balmoral

The whine of the engines over Newcastle
Clouds of death over Windsor castle
But we will not be broken
We will resist and we will win

The three lions roar on
Suddenly the Germans are gone
God save the king
May the empire last a thousand years

The News Of The World

Acid rain and atom bombs
Ashen faces of the dead
Is it that a plane over your head
Radio silent music halls
Radioactive activity from dusk to dawn
And don't you leave the lights on

So the whole thing goes
The news…
The news of the world
Nothing prosaic anymore

Shrapnel flakes and bloody robes
Empty cupboards lined in mould
The children growing very old
Stores without their clientele
Rice and bread for a fortune now
Money's no good anyhow

So the whole thing goes
The news…
The news of the world
Nothing prosaic anymore

So the whole thing goes

The news…
The news of the world
Nothing prosaic anymore

No laughter
Only the morning after

Uncle, She

Uncle, she spreads the disease
Wiping millions in cash and lives
Livelihoods come crashing down
Like bridge made of cheap cement

Uncle, she won't let you do as you please
She's got control over all of your lives
And that pooh bear knows everythin' 'bout you
It's 1984 except it's 2023

Uncle, she's got some people out in camps
And ain't nobody doin' a damn thing 'bout that
Cuz they gotcha money
Cash money in their bloody hands

Uncle, she's talkin' 'bout some bloody revolution
Makin' some old man to be some kind of god king
The world's now feelin' kind of evil
Cuz ain't nobody doin' a damn 'bout…

Uncle, she…
Guess I just can't speak no more

Degenerates To Arms

Degenerates to arms!
The vagabonds, the hustlers, the losers
The stoners, the composers, the posers
Rise up in revolution
Bring on the next stage of evolution
Blood and panic in the streets
Murder, mayhem and madness in the malls
Despair behind every man's four walls
Among the readers of Locke, Kant and Keats
All the rebels rebel against the hounds of hell
Be locked and loaded to toll the bell
Degenerates to arms!

Aux armes les dégénérés!
Les freaks, les chics, les ecclésiastiques
Ceux qui ont les gillets rouges, blues, blancs et jaunes
Nous qui sommes aux profondeurs de la merde
De mer jusqu'au mer
On s'est levé contre l'ennemi
Et tout frère de la révolution est mon ami Aux armes les dégénérés!

Degenerates to arms!
We who have nothing to lose
Because we already lost it all

Those of us with nowhere further to fall
We who have no route left to choose
But that of ideological revolution
Melting into the new age of evolution
Degenerates to arms!

What The Truck Is Going On

They're running through the Trans-Can in north Ontario
Whole country knows now which way they will go
Some taking jabs against the jab in the press
Others jabbing against those against the press

Nobody knows what the truck is going on
And nobody knows where the truck it's going now

People shouting "truck you" to the man upon the hill
Hot tubs and hockey sticks for the storming of the hill
Two years of feeling blue and nothing much to do
So, we just eat each other – no brotherhood anymore

Nobody knows what the truck is going on
And nobody knows where the truck it's going now

What the truck is going on
Where the truck's it headed now
The life we had is trucking gone
It feels like we're not living now

Grim Reaper's at our doors
Barricades block out the empty stores
We've lost our trucking way
It's night even when it's day

Nobody knows what the truck is going on
And nobody knows where the truck it's going now

Nobody knows what the truck is going on
And nobody knows where the truck it's going now

I'm Off To America

I'm getting tired of the old world
I wish to go to the end of the world
In search of a future
And a clean break from the chains of the past
Because life's passing fast

I'm off to America
Land of the free and home of the brave
Well ain't that America
Where the fair lady waits on the shining shore

Mama there's a city on a hill
With shining lights lit by human will
The favorite of merchants
Home of saints and sinners from the world all around
And the treasure they have found

I'm off to America
Land of the free and home of the brave
Well ain't that America
Hugged by the oceans who fight for her love

I'm off to America
Land of the free and home of the brave
Well ain't that America

Nation of nations who've gathered around

I'm off to America
I'll make it in America
I'll be great in America

Vova Is Hungry

Vova is hungry
So hungry he could eat a wheat field
So hungry he could eat a country
He'd like to know if we will yield

He serves polonium tea on a winter's day
Taking you window diving on a summer's day
Del capo al segno they play the capo's tune
While others fix over a nordic rune

See the blood moon rising
Watch the dead men fighting
Millions condemned at the stroke of a pen
As Vova expands the lion's den

Dispatch From Mariupol

They came forth on the twenty-fourth
A golden horde from the east
With their thousands of metal beasts
From the south too they rose
As if from the pits of hell
Ravaging all before them

As the hours passed the bombs grew louder
The song of death humming ever closer
Where there was once laughter there is slaughter
And no luxury like a pint of water
Melitopol fell and terror filled my heart
Thunder now rumbling in the west
Louder, louder, steadily louder

And then the circle closed
Fire from east and west, north and south
Bullets and bombs
Compliments of Muscovy
Platitudes and attitudes
Compliments of the union
Death rained down from land and sea
Fire was seen in the heavens
The buildings burned
Thousands ceased to be

Children came of age in record time
Theater gave way to real-life tragedy

Strewn in the streets are bodies
Parks are now sepulchers
The steeliest of men are in the steel plant
Strangers to the sunlight
With the agonizing in their care
Weakened, fragile bodies

I do not know if we are Masada or Stalingrad
But all will hear of us
From London to Petrograd
Our lands will bloom again
Though we shall not see
Flowers will grow where the invaders fall

When you see that remember this place
Who we were and what happened here
The values you hold dear
Prepare to defend them

And when you do remember us
Victims of the human race

Art And Revolution

Lights, camera, AKTION!!!
No, don't worry
Nobody will die
But Vienna will answer for those she murdered
There will be paint, or maybe it's blood
Art will drown as ugliness crests to a flood
Artists kept in bandage and bondage
Only then can they be free

There will be senseless pictures to make sense of the world
A woman's supple breasts smeared in paint
Her face hidden from a Nikon camera
A naked Vienna exposed to the outside world
Got tired of the Viennese waltz
So went on a Viennese walk
Painted white and painted black
Pale, thin reflection of society's lack of tack
Caught a cab and a handful of stares
But all this was the least of our cares

Blood and milk
Shit and entrails
And all that that entails
Nothing's as smooth as silk
Not in a broken mind

Not among our broken kind

Ah those starry-eyed students
How they shat themselves as we cut ourselves
Marinated in our own waste and sang the great Austrian song
For a while they were but our students
Adrift in our obscenity and immersed in our wrong
They ate the trauma and drank the pain

This world makes one want to cut his head open
And have it all come gushing out
Or should I say pouring onto an empty canvas
Leaving all of our angst out in the open
No boundary left but the final one
No human left inside but the broken one

Give us calamity and give us depravity
Give us silence and give us violence
Give us confusion and give us convolution
But most of all, give us art and revolution

A Song For Hilda

Your voice carried from Manhattan, New York to Manhattan Beach
Ebbets Field was never far out of reach
The Brooklyn drawl announced your arrival
Silence was the harbinger of your departure

Peanuts bagged and hot dogs sold
Your penance was done
And the game was yours to enjoy
"Hilda Is Here" read the sign

Frying pans, ladles and cowbells were your weapons of war
Sadness in the air as the boys went off to war
But you were explosions of joy amidst the atom bombs
A cacophony of life among the many deaths

For a dime you had a very good time
Injected life into a life devoid of life
And though you were nobody's wife
You loved and were loved with a love only sports fans can know

You called your game
Brooklyn knew your name
You were a lonely soldier
And yet, you headed an army

The Dodgers broke your heart once, twice
And then once too many
You were a stranger and yet you were family
You blazed brightly then faded away

Death To The Tsar

Revolution, constitution, retribution
Avenge the blood of our martyrs
Bring on national evolution
Rights for all

One man, one vote
Death to fascism!
Freedom to the people

Let Sarmats rust
Leave the mobiki be
Let the old lands love their new lovers
But let there be cash in the banks
Food in the stores
And lives in our young

No more games of Risk for the Tsar
To hell with the Tsar
Let him rot from within
Drown in his billions
With none left to save him

Only then will the transgression be finished
And peace restored upon the land

Death to tyrants!
Let freedom ring for one and for all
No more sacrifices for vanity and ego
Enough of the past
Let Swan Lake play
Death to the Tsar!

Section Three: Our Internal Struggles

Life has no manual. Each individual is born into a unique set of circumstances that informs the particulars of their individual existence and its struggles. These struggles are both physical and mental but it is the latter which serves as a gold mine for the poet because it so often involves making sense of that which is abstract and formless. One's mental struggles are so often capricious and incoherent that at times one wonders if he has gone irrevocably mad, or on better days, if they are even struggles at all.

Our family and peers are often oblivious and even when their suspicions are roused one is hard-pressed to coherently express the situation. It is here where the bond between art and struggle becomes most apparent because art allows humans to express that which ordinary speech so often fails to. Struggle nurtures art and art itself can be understood as a struggle in its own right. Therefore it can also be said that art nurtures struggle. Meditation on those two thoughts implies that art is a signal of distress. One seldom creates art because all is well in their world or in the world but out of a wish for something or other to be different. Whether one rages against the machine overtly or subtly, the point is that one rages. The machine may be society, the political, industrial or academic classes, or even ourselves. Yet the point remains the same. Herein lies another struggle. Shall we temper our loathing for the status quo for the sake of diplomacy or a desire to avoid conflict? Or is the answer to go all out and create with the bluntest of force? And how much should we share about our inner workings? How vulnerable can the artist be without feeling totally ashamed of his or her nakedness? Artists struggle with this form of self-censorship as well in creating their work. There is also a thought to be spared for the artists that operate in repressive environments. This is a more external struggle whether it be a repressive family or a repressive socio-political environment. But it births other internal struggles like guilt, fear and paranoia. It also builds further resentment which feeds great art but also risks destroying the artist from within.

Artists also struggle with the imaginary mirror that they hold to themselves as they create. Do they like their reflection? Or is there something there that bothers them? In a world in which there is a much more acute awareness of mental health it is easier to spot those warts which are so easily hidden from the outside world. And this is a good thing even if the knowledge can be painful to possess. After all, one can only begin to repair that of which one is aware.

However, not all of the flaws which the artist sees are real. There are things that we come to hate ourselves for that simply do not bother others. Perhaps they even like these qualities in us. But we are children of today's increasingly superficial society where we feel we must airbrush even the tiniest perceived imperfections. We are the self-conscious generation and the artist, whose life's work involves deep self-examination, suffers doubly for it.

Inner struggles are also influenced by outside factors of

course. Simple change itself unsettled people in ways we are only now truly starting to understand. This is exacerbated by the fact that changes happen much faster and more abruptly in today's world than in generations past. This trend can only be expected to continue as technology advances further. In the world of 2022-23 though, there is more than just change which plays on our minds. We are coming out of the deadliest pandemic in a generation, or so we think. We also live in an era where we stand on the brink of world War between the United States and its allies, and China and Russia with theirs. In democracies, people watch the slow erosion of respect for liberal-democratic institutions. In autocracies, the promised stability and efficiency never arrived and never will. We live in a bleak and potentially transformative moment in history where life is taking on a steadily more foreboding and onerous tone. Food and fuel prices skyrocket while wages stagnate and milestones like home ownership become pipe dreams. The artists see these phenomena and despair for their generation. This despair is expressed through their art. In so doing, they live their struggles and those of their peers.

Struggles of individual existence take many forms and are expressed in the beauty all around us. The Moonlight Sonata, the Divine Comedy, Starry Night and the Statue of Liberty were all born of struggle and express struggle in some overt or covert way. Somewhere struggles of love and anger, others against repressive systems and constraining dogmas, and others for control over the mind. Some despaired until they could no longer. Others did so until laughter won them over as they saw their lives for the tragicomedy that it was. Whether they questioned their place in the world or the world's place in them, the great artists of the past all struggled within themselves to give birth to the individual greatness that lingered within. Be it depression, anxiety, melancholy or some other existential malaise, the reality is that the art covering our world was informed and continues to be informed by internal struggles. This is true of my art form as well, as the ensuing poetry will attest to.

The Panicked Worker

I'm falling out of love with life
Everything's gone meh
Not even hobbies matter
Just grey zones in my life

Exercise does nothing
A few minutes rush
Then comes the crash
And the dark, painful hush

I really am all alone
Just me and my phone
Just me and my thoughts
Steadily more demented

I shiver like winter on a summer's night
Thinking of the day ahead
The angry emails and tense meetings
I don't want to wake up tomorrow

I can't even cry
Just don't want to be awake
But panic pilfers my blessed sleep
As I slowly continue to die

I just want to disappear

Steal away from it all
Panic sets in as day begins to fall
My torment begins all over again

Force feed myself breakfast
Gobble, gobble very fast
And I just want to throw up
Can't death just hurry up

Eight o'clock comes and my body tenses up
Tears well up but never fall
But still I lose control of it all

I run to the bathroom for shelter
I hate it all

I just want to be free
But salvation's a lie
Freedom's just a final goodbye

The Inner Critic

It's never gonna be okay
You'll never find your love
They'll leave you feeling grey
Nothing's overrated like love

You will lose that job
You know you're a failure
You bombed that meeting
You know you botched the project

Hide all you like
Pretend it's all fine
Affirmations are a waste
Your dreams have gone to waste

Gorge on candy and ice cream
It's easier that cutting your veins
Sometimes it's better to fade away
Burnout means ashes to be swept away

Most kill themselves slowly
Few dare do it quickly
Does your hand tremble
Do your lips quiver

The Great Disappointment

The day fast approaches
Dies Irae!
The wind is blowing
The night is day
The wonders begin
I've claimed the mountain
I see the top
The top of the world
I've sailed the oceans
Avenged the drowned sevenfold
Reaching land at last
And alas
It is not exhilarating
There is no thrill
It all felt banal
When I crossed the canal
No trumpet calls
No golden lights
Just a great disappointment
I have achieved nothing
I have opened no pearly gates
I am just another Millerite
Dazed and confused
Still as dysthymic as before
Head in hands
Living the dream
And greatly disappointed

The Pill

Welcome to the fear chamber
You know it as Planet Earth
Hear the truth for what it's worth
Step out of the echo chamber
Take the pill if you will

Come and know the dark comedy
Be penetrated by the dark light
And find the world's a divine comedy
As you curl up in fright
Take the pill if you will

Take up residence between dystopia and disturbia
It's not like there's someplace else to go
But there's knowledge they don't want you to know
And so there's a shroud to cover ya
Take the pill if you will

Another Day

Early rise and early go
Off to trudge in blowing snow
It's just another day of feeling barely alive
Recall when good times rolled
You master of the universe or so you were told
It seems so long ago now

That's just the way it goes
Dreams go missing and then no one knows
There are no suspects and there are no leads
You trudge a path and know not where it leads

You live your square space
With other members of the human race
In this crowd you're just another face
Another so and so who lives then dies

You bring home bacon and a few things more
Exchanged for hours of eternal bore
You're just another hamster on a wheel

That's just the way it goes
Dreams go missing and then no one knows
There are no suspects and there are no leads
You trudge a path and know not where it leads

Until I Come Home

In a run-down neighbourhood in a dead-end street
Lives a mother always staying on her feet
Slaving away for the thousandth day
With one eye on the dusty way
And a teardrop in her eye
She sighs a heavy sigh
Broken by worried nights until I come home

In the garage of a rundown house
Works the broken woman's longtime spouse
Nostalgic 'bout the good ol' days
For he has lost his universe
Of fishing trips and junipers
And a teardrop in his eye
He sighs a heavy sigh
Broken by worried nights until I come home

Been away for an eternity
Living in it seems another galaxy
They are living on a prayer
Along a dusty road of a long-forsaken town
I count the footsteps until I come home
I'm coming home

Franz To His Father

You are my father
And I, your son
Your little bother
Your curse
Your shame
Your one to blame

You are fire
And I, water
You are success
And I, failure
Freezing on a cold, dark night
Asking what gave you the right

You are my tormentor
And I, your disappointment
You are the judge
And I, the convict
Condemned to die in the river
Without so much as a whisper

You are the specimen
And I, the laughing stock
You won at love
And I settled for the brothels

One-night stands
Secreting angst through my glands

You are the giant
And I, the insect
To be crushed at will
For a momentary thrill
A loathsome thing
Unworthy of your golden ring

You are the beast of the water
And I the frail, sickly swimmer
You are the shark
And I, the minnow
Weak and inferior
Both interior and exterior

You have golden factories
And I, insurance papers
You are fit for a captain's chair
And I, fit for discarding in a quarry
Knife in my heart
From a man without a heart

Sorry you hate me
Sorry you broke me
I wish I was better
I beg for forgiveness

Franz

Life As Solitaire

Crimsons and clovers
Angels and wedding bells
Chiming a lullaby
For those that are loners
Don't tells and show 'n' tells
The sun shines for us all

Can you hear you a melody
Can you sing you a harmony
Is life better with company
Or better done solitary

Raindrops and teardrops
Lilacs and daffodils
Barley and hops
Shadows and highlights
Star lights and moonlight
Piercing black skies

Can you hear you a melody
Can you sing you a harmony
Is life better with company
Or better done solitary

Everything's temporary
Nothing's forever

West wind is solitary
Forever and ever

Everything's temporary
Nothing's forever
West wind is solitary
Forever and ever

Can you hear you a melody
Can you sing you a harmony
Is life better with company
Or better done solitary

A Note For A Friend

Roll your boulder up the hill
Triumphantly and tragically
Devoid of a magic pill
Comically and candidly
Laughing at and loving your fate
Till death should take you on a date

And you've become stardust once more
But for now one day more
Seeking your invincible summer
In this darkest winter
Accompanied but alone
Weary to the bone

Chasing phantoms in the night sky
Till the vial of vril should go dry
From chasing glory or chasing her
Becoming someone else in hopes of having her
Only to find she lusted for another
While you lusted in vain

Heart and soul shattered from pain
And yet you smile
As if you only walked a mile
For you know this was our lot

We are of the system
Kind of heart it is not
But it is the system
And we, absurdly are its heroes
Absurd, comic heroes
Living lives without appeal
With wounds that never heal

Dead In The Dead Of Night

Long days and even longer faces
Cold days and even colder cases
Forgotten dreams that turned to ash
Feel like you're gonna crash
Mind's slow
And that's got you feeling low

The tears hide in evening black skies
No moon or stars above
Somewhere an angel meant for you cries
Wishing to fall in love

The castle begins to fall down
The cracks inside got you feeling so down
You pine for moonshine
To drink the pain away
But you eat it all instead
It's for the best that way

The lines upon your face
Disguise themselves in the dead of night
With no more strength to fight
You fall out of the race
The red eyes set to cry
Mask themselves in this lonely night
Tempted into saying your goodbyes
But you curl up in fright

All Is Transitory

Everyone is transitory
Here today
Gone tomorrow
Smoke in the wind
Flash in the pan
Rotating in and out
In and out of my life
Round and round they go
To places I do not know
Out and about
Free as birds

From Ottawa to Florida
Alive today
Tomorrow dead
I too am smoke
Curling above your shoulder
Dissipating slowly or quickly
According to your taste
  I too am transitory
  Nothing but a symbol
  Drawn on high
  By the Eternal Feminine

An Abstraction

Is there vril in that magic little pill
Something there to make you superhuman
Übermensch or something strange
Some noble, thin, white human

Is there energy in your universe
Summoned through the power of will
Colours and stars in the multiverse
Electric and eclectic levitate soul

Are you of the coming master race
Subterranean souls who vanish without a trace
Who live where the black sun shines
Deluded and convoluted

Or are you simply esoteric
Proudly a heretic
Druid in persuasion
Ghost-like in contemplation

Pirouettes In Shadows

Between newspapers and half-smoked cigarettes
A dreamer dreams of amber greens
White papers turn to atom bombs
Of desire painted sure white stains
A mind keeps turning pirouettes
Deep within its own shadows

The diver drowns in deeper depths
Poor pup purrs – puddles of pain
A Nordic winter chills his veins
Checkmate coming!
Nothing to do but resign

And melt away as my season slowly dies
A pen, a gun, a broken dream
A helpless, hopeless artsy scream
Angst spreading like cancer
Eating away what was once a dancer
A mind keeps turning pirouettes
Deep within its own shadows

Afterword

All around us there is struggle. Our lives are bookended by struggle. Life begins with the struggle of a mother in labour and it ends with the agony of a dying body. In between there is more struggle as you all know. I hope that the preceding array of poetry examines struggle from as many angles as is possible within one fairly short book. I hope there were emotions and epiphanies even if they were different from whatever it was that I intended in each particular piece. A beautiful quality of any kind of art is that it can be understood and experienced in different ways. Perhaps attempting to cultivate a specific emotion is a struggle but if the reader responds differently than expected this is not a failure.

In the foreword for my last collection I discussed the idea of the creative victory. This comes through struggle as well. Producing new art takes toil and the chutzpah to believe that you have something of value. Overcoming the voice trying to convince you of the contrary is the creative victory. Winning it also requires creating pieces informed by your own struggle. This adds a strong flavour of authenticity but it also requires profound exploration of the parts of you that would rather not know. Therefore the creative victory is also a victory over the self. It is born of internal struggle. Art is born of your labour as you were born of your mother's. Producing art requires drinking pain just like cultivating a strong physique does. Moreover, both endeavours are more than just overcoming challenges. These are heroic deeds.

My point here is not to be self-congratulatory, at least not entirely. I believe we often fail to stop and congratulate ourselves for our little acts of heroism. Instead, I wanted to highlight the hint of the heroic that exists within us as humans. A great tragedy in our shared history is that many will live their lives without ever having uncovered this truth. Of those that do, only a subset will accept it. Tragic indeed.

It takes an understanding of struggle and how it manifests in our lives to understand and acquaint ourselves with the hero that exists within us. Some struggles are public and epic, and others quiet and seemingly uninteresting. Notice the word I just injected there. Our struggles seem uninteresting and unimportant, and yet exploring them further allows us to see them as our own private epic, no less compelling that of your neighbours or historical figures of which you have read. This is why I chose to centre this whole collection around the theme of struggle. It was not an act of masochism dressed as artistic writing, but an oblique affirmation of life and of our innate heroic moments.

The immigrant father who juggles a new culture and language with taking a job objectively beneath him or the single mother who works two jobs whilst simultaneously playing mother and father both struggle heroically. Through their sacrifice the world of their offspring is improved and hopefully through them the world of many others. These acts of heroic struggle may not be visible to most or understood as heroic by the strugglers themselves, and yet examining them inspires a renewed sense of faith in human possibilities and human decency. The lover whose heart was smashed into a million pieces by being lied to or simply ignored also struggles heroically. So does the one who suddenly became unemployed and still finds a way forward.

The one who bucked convention and chose to explore the world rejecting the comfort of the nine to five also struggles against the doubters, both internal and external. The one who works a comfortable nine to five also finds struggle under the veneer of stability. In fact, they can be the ones who struggle the most, and the most quietly.

Quiet struggles are the ones that receive the least attention and yet they are the most fascinating. One can smile, work normally and yet feel on the brink of calamity, all without so much as a whisper. Slowly the bile stews away, unassuming and devoid of fanfare. And then, as the threshold is quietly reached, the storm finally comes. It is sudden and spectacular in its fury. Everything becomes bleak. Everything turns dark. You come to question everything. You remain forgiving with all but yourself. The object of your loathing is you. You become the bug once named Gregor Samsa. You are guilty and you are to blame, a putrid thing in your own mind.

Every mistake is an affirmation of your inadequacy. Every bumbled social interaction, a sign that perhaps you should not be around people. Are you even human at all? The circles around your eyes grow darker as the haze before you grows steadily grainier and less intelligible. Life is then reduced to an algorithm, a steady stream of predictable movements timed to such perfection that you convince yourself that you are devoid of all sense of agency. The time you wake up, the time you log on for work, the time you log off from work, (save for the emails you continue to respond to late into the night) the time you go to bed, all so neatly programmed that you may as well be robotic. That is not a life, merely an existence and you know it to be true but you insist on this paradigm because you are of the system and for the system. You were taught to serve all but yourself. You were reared to give to all but yourself. You know but you suppress it because there are bills to pay and appearances to keep. You suppress until you finally break. Your limbs become smouldering ruins, your mind bombed out by HIMARS far away. You long for someone to speak to, someone who understands but nobody truly gets it or so you think. You want so badly to tell someone that you feel trapped and that your existence feels hollow and pointless. You want adventure. You want a deeper purpose. You want a legacy. But you also want comfort and stability and the competing priorities tear you limb by limb.

I know how all this feels. I am making my way through those forests as I write this. Add to this the fear that your youth is seeping through your hands with you having not really enjoyed it and you have a cocktail for a crisis. And add a corrosive sense of isolation and all becomes still more bleak. All the other crises lead you to withdraw from the world. And so, you feel more and more alone. When I chose the name "Returning From Exile" for this collection, I meant more than simply returning to somewhat normal life post-pandemic, but also a return from a more personal exile which the last few paragraphs have been referring to. This collection comes from darkness and represents the longing for a light at the end of the long, dark tunnel of doubt and anxiety and their associates. I hope it speaks to the downtrodden, the lonely, the stressed, the anxious and the disaffected. I hope it speaks to and not for them. They deserve, as I do, to speak for themselves but for those who cannot then let it speak on their behalf. Let this collection also represent the will to confront the dragon and find the heroism that exists within us even in our darkest hour. Let it prompt the confrontation with our struggles that allows us to see ourselves for the heroic beings that deep down inside, we know we really are.

The idea of returning from exile also means returning to ourselves. Sometimes, the correct and heroic thing is something associated with the polar opposite, turn and run. It is a waste of our struggle to shackle ourselves to that which destroys us. There is bravery sometimes in cutting bait, opinions and attempts to box you in be damned. Life is one, and we all deserve to do something that brings us joy. We all deserve to go home to ourselves. We all deserve to return from exile. And with that comes my final exhortation before closing this chapter in my literary journey: make the journey, make Aliyah, especially those of my generation. Do not lose the bulk of your twenties trying to be that which you are not. These are supposed to be the beautiful years, not the lost years. Fall in love, go out, travel if you can, write, sing, dance, play. I deeply regret not doing those things before but at least I can start now. At least I know my true vocation now in which you are partaking. I also now understand the value of time in a new, more polished sense. There is a greater clarity in what is urgent, and what is not. I guess you could say that I am slowly making my way back from Babylon to the land restored from war, to my own personal Zion. I hope you claw your way back to yours as well.